# SILVER BURDETT SCIENCE

## Centennial Edition

## GEORGE G. MALLINSON
Distinguished Professor
of Science Education
Western Michigan University

## JACQUELINE B. MALLINSON
Associate Professor of Science
Western Michigan University

## WILLIAM L. SMALLWOOD
Head, Science Department
The Community School
Sun Valley, Idaho

## CATHERINE VALENTINO
Former Director of Instruction
North Kingstown School Department
North Kingstown, Rhode Island

## SILVER BURDETT COMPANY
**MORRISTOWN, NJ**
Atlanta, GA • Cincinnati, OH • Dallas, TX • Northfield, IL •
San Carlos, CA • Agincourt, Ontario

# SILVER BURDETT

# SCIENCE

## Centennial Edition

GEORGE G. MALLINSON

JACQUELINE B. MALLINSON

WILLIAM L. SMALLWOOD

CATHERINE VALENTINO

# THE SILVER BURDETT ELEMENTARY SCIENCE PROGRAM
## 1-6 PUPILS' BOOKS
### AND
## TEACHERS' EDITIONS LEVELS K-6

ISBN 0-382-13102-9

# CONTENTS

# 1. Learning About Our World

You have five senses.

You use your senses
    to see
    to hear
    to smell
    to taste
    to feel.

You use your eyes to see.
You can see near and far.

Look at the rock when it is far from you.

How does the rock look?

Move the rock closer to you.

How does the rock look now?

Look at the rock with a hand lens.

How does the rock look now?

You can see many shapes.

How many shapes do you see here?

You can see many colors.

How many colors do you see here?

Animals also use eyes to see.

Find the eyes on each animal.

You use your ears to hear.

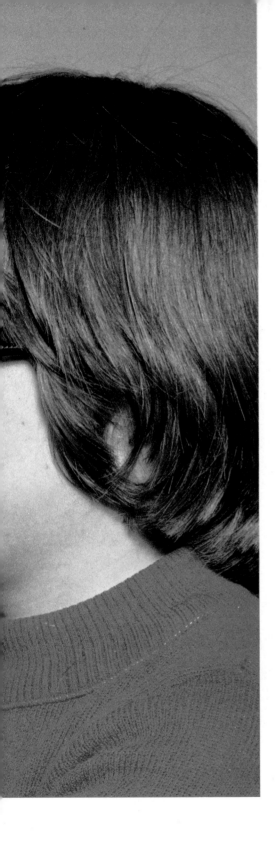

There are many different sounds.
Some sounds are loud.

Some sounds are soft.

Try this.

What sound do you hear?

Where is the sound coming from?

Point to the sound.

Animals also use ears to hear.

Find the ears on each animal.

You use your nose to smell.

Some things smell good.

Some things smell bad.

How do these things smell?

Try this.

Name the foods you smell.

Animals also use a nose to smell.

Find the nose on each animal.

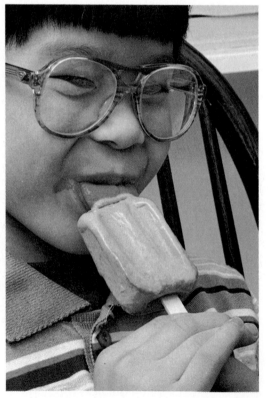

You use your tongue to taste.
Foods have different tastes.

# How do these foods taste?

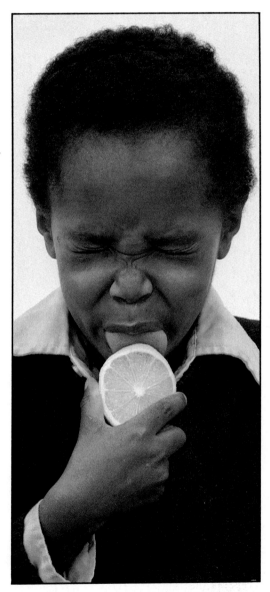

17

You use your skin to feel.
Some things feel cold.
Some things feel warm.

Some things feel hard.

Some things feel soft.

Find the things that feel hard.

Find the things that feel soft.

19

Some things feel rough.
Some things feel smooth.
Find the things that feel rough.
Find the things that feel smooth.

20

Try this.

Feel different things.

Tell how they feel.

# Check It Now

## WORDS TO KNOW

How do these things feel?

Match the pictures with the words.

hot     smooth     rough     cold

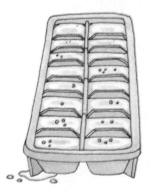   

Which word do you need?

Use each word once.

nose     ears     eyes     skin     tongue

You use your ___ to see.

You use your ___ to smell.

You use your ___ to hear.

You use your ___ to taste.

You use your ___ to feel.

## IDEAS TO KNOW

Match the pictures with the words.

see

hear

taste

feel

smell

## USING IDEAS

Make a book.

Find things that feel rough.

Find things that feel smooth.

Find things that feel soft or hard.

Glue two things that feel the same on each page.

Make a cover.

# 2. Many Kinds of Plants

There are many kinds of plants.

How many kinds do you see here?

Some plants are big.

Some plants are small.

Plants have many shapes.

Plants also have many colors.

What colors do you see here?

Many plants have three main parts.

They have roots.

They have stems.

They have leaves.

The boy is holding a plant.

Find the three main parts.

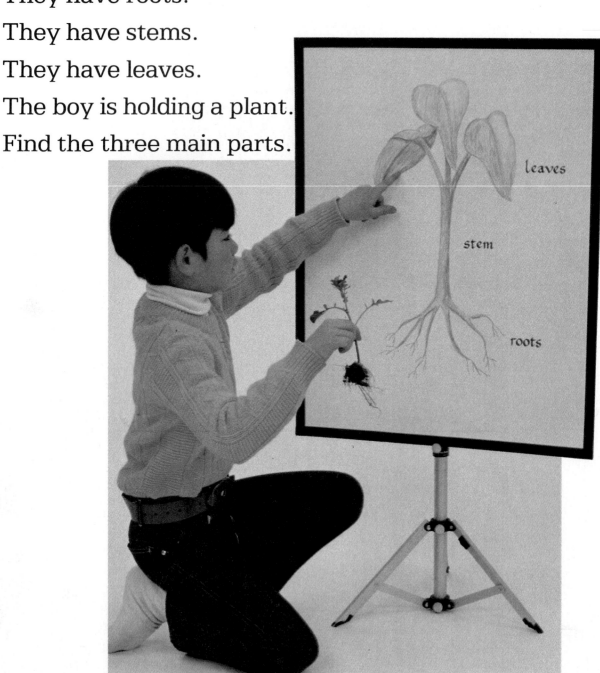

The roots of these plants are different.

How are they different?

Leaves are different shapes.

Leaves are different sizes.

How are these leaves different?

Stems can be long or short.

Stems can be soft or hard.

How are these stems different?

Look at some leaves.

Look at the colors.

Look at the shapes.

Look at the sizes.

Find leaves that look the same.

Put them in a pile.

How many piles did you make?

Plants need some things to live.
Most plants need soil to grow.
They need air and water.
Most plants need light.

Some plants grow indoors.

They need special care.

How is this child taking care of the plant?

Many plants grow from seeds.

Each kind of plant has its own kind of seed.

Try this.

Plant two kinds of seeds.

Water them.

Will the plants be different?

Watch and see.

Plants grow in many places.
Some plants grow in soil.
Other plants grow in water.
Look at the pictures.
How are these places different?

Some plants grow in strange places.

Where are these plants growing?

People use plants for food.

Can you name these foods?

People use plants for other things.

How do people use these plants?

# Check It Now

**WORDS TO KNOW**

What are these things?

Match the pictures with the words.

stems     roots     leaves

 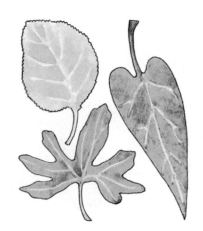 

Which word do you need?

Use each word once.

soil    seeds    food    three

Many plants grow from _____ .

Many plants grow in _____ .

Plants give us many kinds of _____ .

Many plants have _____ main parts.

## IDEAS TO KNOW

Which comes first?

Put these pictures in order.

Which things come from plants?

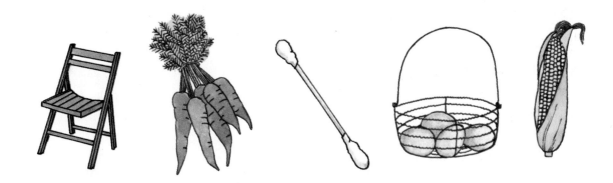

## USING IDEAS

Put carrot tops in a pan of water.

Look at them after a few days.

Do you see any changes?

# 3. Many Kinds of Animals

There are many kinds of animals.

They do not all look the same.

How are they different?

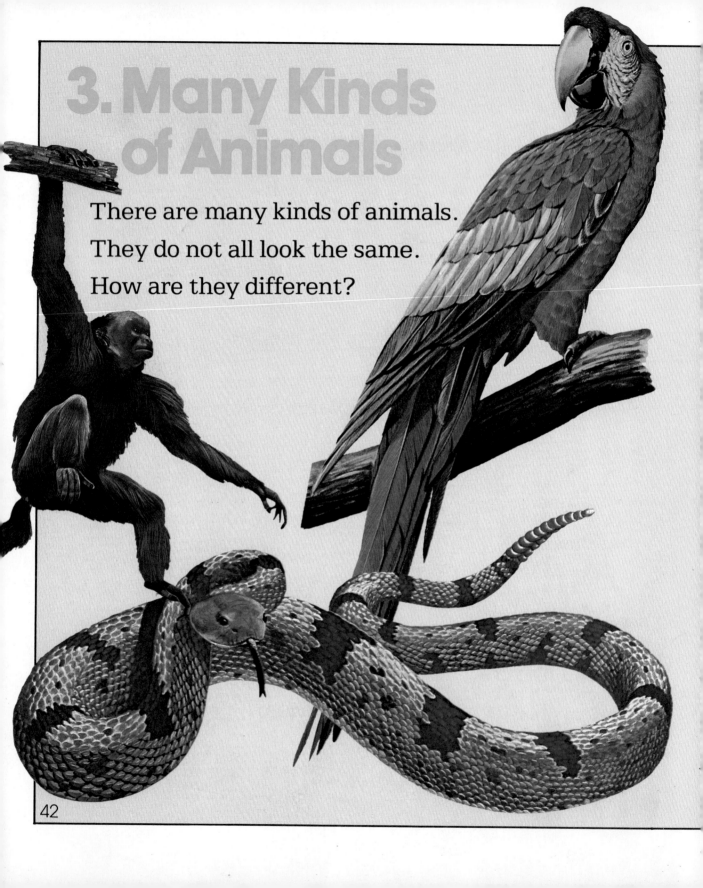

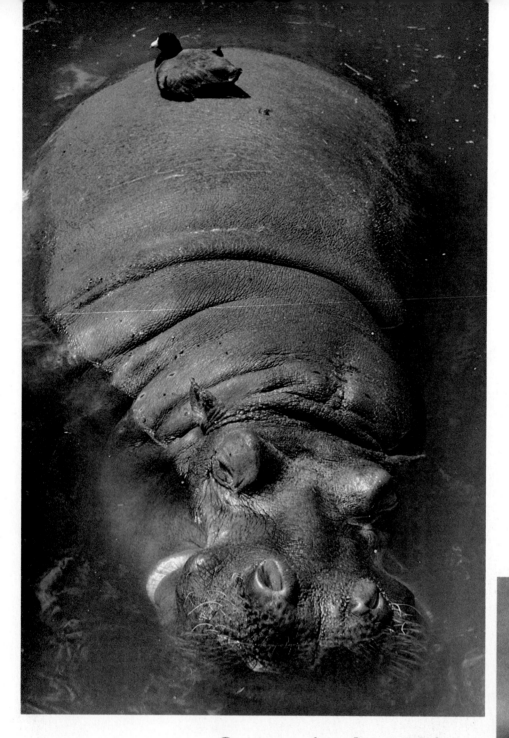

Some animals are big.
Some animals are small.

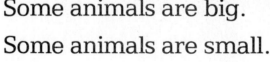

44

Which animals are big?

Which animals are small?

Some animals have fur.
Some animals have feathers.

Some animals have a hard shell.

Which animals here have a hard shell?

What do the other animals have?

Animals can move.

They move in many ways.

Some animals run.

Some animals hop.

Some animals swim.

Other animals fly.

Some animals move in other ways.

How do these animals move?

Many baby animals look like their parents.

Do these babies look like their parents?

How are they the same?

How are they different?

These baby animals do not look like their parents.

How are they different?

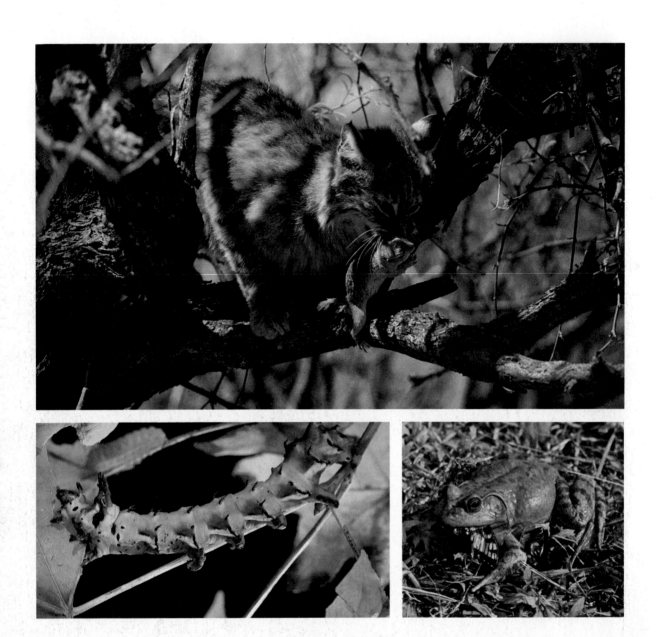

Animals eat many things.

Some animals eat plants.

Some animals eat other animals.

What are these animals eating?

Animals catch food in many ways.

How are these animals catching their food?

Animals need more than food.
They need water to drink.
Some also live in the water.

Animals need air.

All animals need air to breathe.

Some animals move in the air.

Animals need a place to live.

They live in many kinds of places.

Where do these animals live?

Make a home for a pet.

Give your pet water and food.

What else does your pet need?

Some animals make good pets.

People must take care of pets.

How are people taking care of these pets?

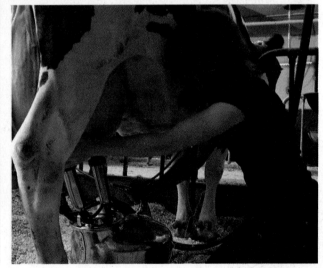

People use animals in different ways.

We get food from animals.

We also get clothing from animals.

Some animals do work.

How are these animals helping?

Try this.

Cut out pictures that show how we use animals.

Put the pictures into groups like this.

# Check It Now

How do these animals move?

Match the pictures with the words.

hopping     walking     flying     running

## IDEAS TO KNOW

Look at the picture.

Name two animals that do not belong.

Name one animal with feathers.

## USING IDEAS

Can you be an elephant?

Swing your trunk from side to side.

Can you be a rabbit?

Hop here and there.

What other animals can you be?

63

# 4. Using Colors, Shapes, and Sizes

You use colors.

You use shapes.

You use sizes.

You use them to tell about things.

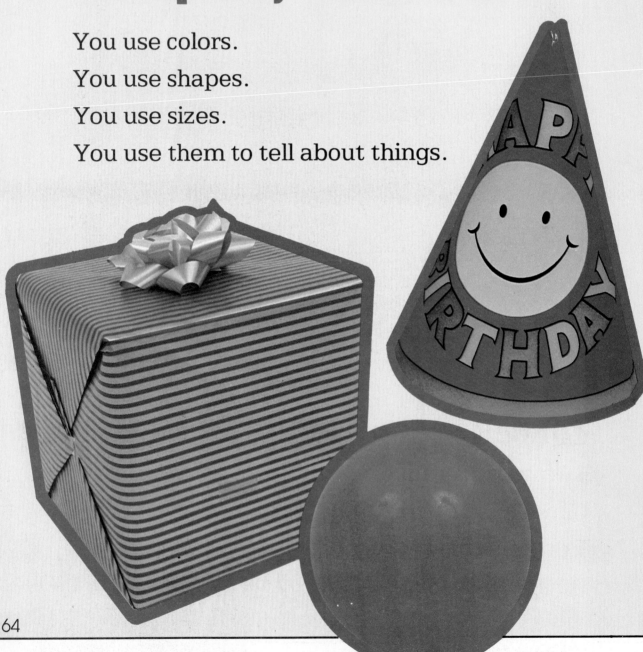

You can see many colors.

Colors help you learn.

They help you tell about things.

The hats in the picture are different.

How are they different?

Look at the picture.

Name things that are the same color.

Name things that are different colors.

Try this.

Mix some colors.

Try different colors.

What colors can you make?

Now try this.

What will the blue color do?

You can see shapes.

You can feel shapes.

You can use shapes.

Shapes help you learn.

What shapes do you see in the picture?

Look at the picture.

The children are looking at some things.

Name things that have the same shape.

Name things that have different shapes.

Try this.

Put some shapes together.

Can you make a picture?

What picture did you make?

Some things are big.

Some things are small.

Sizes help you learn about things.

They help you tell about things.

Tell about the shoes.

How are they different?

Clothes come in different sizes.

People are different sizes.

Look at the pictures.

How does the hat fit?

How does the dress fit?

Some things are tall.

Some things are short.

Look at the pictures.

Which animal is taller?

74

BE CAREFUL.
SOME SNAKES
ARE HARMFUL.

Some snakes are long.

Some snakes are longer.

Look at the pictures.

Which snake is longest?

How long is the table?

Get some straws.

Put them in a line on the table.

Count the straws.

How many straws did you use?

How tall is the boy?

Tape the straws next to a person.

Count the straws.

How many straws did you use?

Things take up space.

Some things take up a lot of space.

Some things take up less space.

What is in the boxes?

Which one takes up the most space?

# Check It Now

**WORDS TO KNOW**

How are the trucks alike?

How are the trucks different?

Which word do you need?

Use each word once.

tall     long     red     short

The       is ____.

The       is ____.

The       is ____.

The       is ____.

## IDEAS TO KNOW

Look at the picture.

What shapes do you see?

What colors do you see?

## USING IDEAS

Use some paper clips to find out how long things are.

How long is a pencil?

How long is this book?

Which one is longer?

# 5. Living and Not Living

Look at the pictures.

Which things are living?

Which things are not living?

Animals are living things.
Plants are living things.
People are living things.
Living things grow.

Trees are living things that grow.

These pictures show the same tree.

How do you know this tree grew?

Are these things living?

Will they grow?

Things that are not living do not grow.

Many living things can move on their own.

Animals are living things that move.

Birds can fly.

Dogs can run.

Insects can hop.

Many things cannot move on their own.

They need help to move from place to place.

These things are not living.

What helps these things move?

Try this.

Make a boat.

Make your boat move from place to place.

What helps your boat move?

Is your boat a living thing?

Plants and animals need many things to live.

They need food to help them grow.

They also need air and water.

Look at the picture.

What living things do you see?

What do they need to live?

Get two plants that are alike.

Put both plants in sunlight.

Water one.

Do not water the other.

What happens after a few days?

Things that are not living can be anywhere.

A rock is not living.

These are moon rocks.

They do not need food, air, or water.

Living things make new living things.

Plants make seeds.

Seeds grow into new plants.

Dogs have puppies.

Birds lay eggs.

Baby birds hatch from eggs.

Find pictures of things that are living.

Find pictures of things that are not living.

Make a chart like this.

# Check It Now

**WORDS TO KNOW**

Look at each picture.

Which are living?

Which are not living?

Which word do you need?

Use each word once.

air    rock    living    grow

A tree is a ___ thing.

A ___ is not a living thing.

Things that are not living do not ___.

Animals need water, food, and ___ to stay alive.

## IDEAS TO KNOW

Look at the picture.

Point to three things that are living.

Point to three things that are not living.

## USING IDEAS

Go on a walk.

Find things that are living.

Find things that are not living.

Tell how they are different.

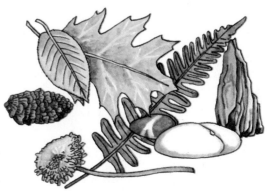

# 6. Moving Things

Many things move.

Cars and trains move.

Animals move.

People move.

How do these things move?

We can see when things are moved.

They are in different places.

Look at the two pictures.

What things are in different places?

We can feel things move.

Which child can feel things move?

We can hear things move.

Can this boy tell the chair is moving?

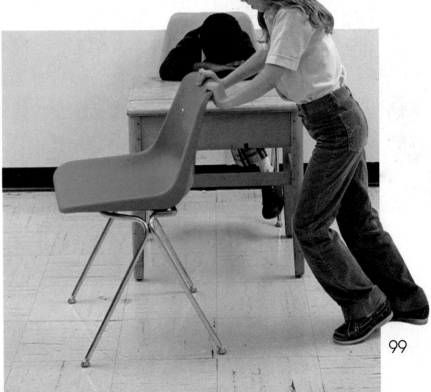

Things move in many ways.

Some things move up and down.

Some things roll and spin.

Some things float.

How do these things move?

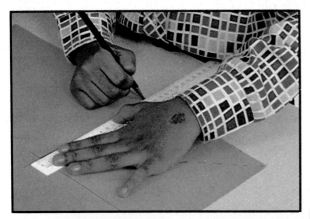

Look at the pictures.

Make a paper pinwheel.

Blow on the pinwheel.

Does it move?

What makes it move?

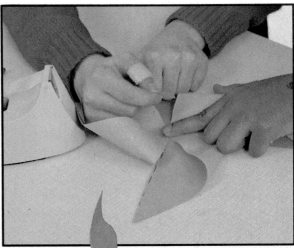

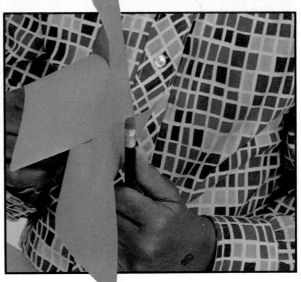

Things move at different speeds.

Some things move fast.

Some things move slowly.

How do these things move?

People move things in different ways.

They can push or pull things.

Sometimes they lift things.

How is the girl moving the dog?

Machines help us move things.
These are simple machines.

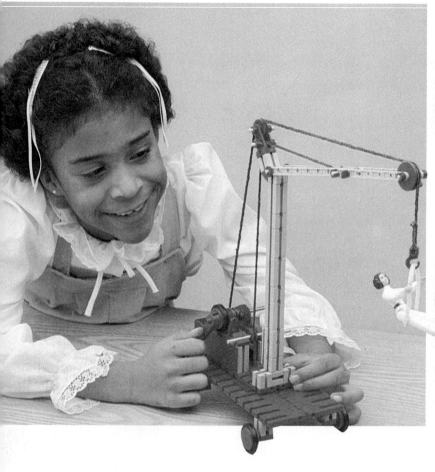

How do these machines help to move things?

Machines help us do work.

They make work easier.

How are these machines helping?

Make a machine.

Get a box.

Tape two straws to the box.

Put four wheels on the box.

What did you make?

Can your machine move things?

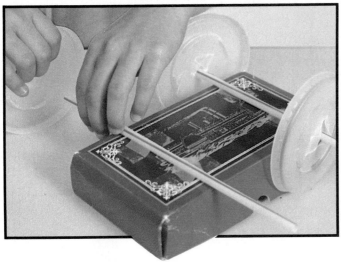

# Check It Now

**WORDS TO KNOW**

What are they doing?

Match the pictures with the words.

    lift      push      pull

Which word do you need?

Use each word once.

    rolls      spins     floats     slowly     fast

The  moves ____.

The  moves ____.

The  ____ down the hill.

The  ____ in the sky.

The  ____ on the floor.

108

## IDEAS TO KNOW

What makes these things move?

Look at the pictures.

Tell how you use each machine.

## USING IDEAS

Pretend you are an airplane.

Fly round and round.

Make your engine roar.

# 7. Our Earth

The earth is made of many things.

What things do you see in the pictures?

Which of these things are part of the earth?

The earth is round.

It is shaped like a ball.

A globe looks like the earth.

How are these other things like the earth?

The earth looks like this from space.

Can you see the water?

Can you see the land?

What else do you see?

The land is made of rock and soil.

Some rocks are big.

Some rocks are small.

Rocks have many shapes.

Some rocks are flat.

Some rocks are round.

What other shapes do you see?

Find at least three kinds of soil.

Look at each kind.

What do you see?

How are they the same?

How are they different?

The land is not the same in all places.

In some places the land is high.

In other places the land is low.

In some places there are hills.
In other places the land is flat.

Water covers much of the earth.

Most of the water is in the oceans.

Some of the water is in lakes and ponds.

There is also water in streams and rivers.

Some places are covered with ice.

Ice is made of water.

There is water in the air.

There is also water in clouds.

Name other places where water is found.

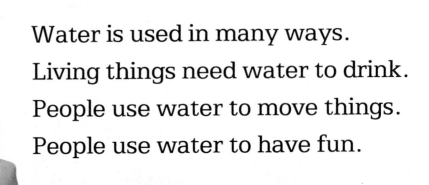

Water is used in many ways.

Living things need water to drink.

People use water to move things.

People use water to have fun.

Sometimes water can be harmful.

Too much water causes floods.

It can wear away the land.

Water can also become dirty.

What causes these things to happen?

Try this.

What happens?

How does water change the land?

How has water changed this land?

Air covers the earth.

We cannot see air.

We cannot taste air.

How do you know there is air in the picture?

Air is used in many ways.

Living things need air to live.

People use air to dry their clothes.

People use air to move things.

People use air to have fun.

Air can be harmful.

Sometimes air moves very fast.

Air can also become dirty.

How is the air in the pictures harmful?

# Check It Now

**WORDS TO KNOW**

What are these things?

Match the pictures with the words.

soil    hills    flood    clouds    globe

Which word do you need?

Use each word once.

oceans    air    round    land

The earth is ____ .

The ____ is made of rock and soil.

Most of the water on the earth is in the ____ .

Living things need ____ to breathe.

## IDEAS TO KNOW

Draw a picture about each sentence.

- The earth is made of high land and low land.
- Some places on the earth are covered with ice.
- People need water.
- Air can become dirty.

Water is used in many ways.

How is water used in each picture?

## USING IDEAS

Air can lift things.

Put a balloon on a table.

Put a book on top of it.

Blow up the balloon.

What happens?

# 8. Looking at the Sky

The sky changes from day to night.

What do you see in the daytime?

What do you see at night?

How is the sky different?

The sun rises early in the morning.

It shines all day.

Sometimes clouds block the sun.

Then we cannot see the sun.

The sun sets at night.

The sky gets darker as the sun goes down.

Soon we cannot see the sun.

Everything looks dark.

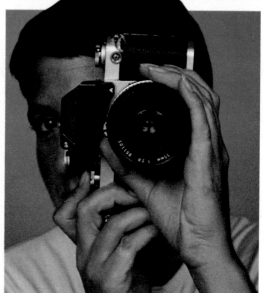

The sun is very important.

It gives us light.

Light from the sun strikes the earth.

Some of this light changes to heat.

During the day the sun warms the earth.

Look at the pictures.

How do you know light changed to heat?

The sky does not look the same at night.

We can see the moon and stars at night.

The moon is the biggest thing in the night sky.

It is smaller than the sun.

But it looks as big as the sun.

This is because it is closer to the earth.

Try this.

Get two balls.

Which ball looks bigger?

Do this.

Does the small ball look bigger now?

Do this.

Which ball looks bigger now?

The moon does not give off its own light.

It is like the earth.

It gets light from the sun.

Light from the sun bounces off the moon.

The moon does not always look the same.

It seems to change its shape.

How has the moon changed in the pictures?

Go into a dark room.

Shine a light on a mirror.

What happens?

Hold a ball in the dark room.

Does it give off light?

Shine the light on the ball.

Think of the ball as the moon.

How is it like the moon?

What would the light be?

People have walked on the moon.

They picked up rocks and soil.

They brought them back to the earth.

These things helped us learn more about the moon.

The moon is different from the earth.

The moon does not have air or water.

The surface is rough.

There are high mountains.

There are deep craters.

At night we see many stars.

Stars are like the sun.

They give off their own light.

Stars are very big.

But they look small.

This is because stars are very far away.

Some stars form pictures in the sky.
This is the Big Dipper.
What does it look like?

# Check It Now

**WORDS TO KNOW**

Look at the pictures.

Match the pictures with the words.

    day        clouds      Big Dipper      night

Which word do you need?

Use each word once.

    light      moon     heat     sun

The ____ gives us light.

Some sunlight changes into ____ .

The ____ is smaller than the sun.

Stars give off their own ____ .

## IDEAS TO KNOW

Which sentence describes each picture?

You see stars in the sky at night.
You see the sun in the sky at night.

The moon warms the earth.
The sun warms the earth.

## USING IDEAS

- The moon seems to change its shape.
  It does not always look the same.
  Draw two of its shapes.

- Make a sunshine book.
  Draw five sunshine pictures.
  Write a sentence about each picture.
  Make a cover.

# 9. You and Weather

Look at the pictures.

Tell what the weather is like.

Is it rainy, snowy, cloudy, sunny?

These words tell about the weather.

There are many kinds of weather.

Weather is always changing.

It can be warm or cold.

It can be wet or dry.

The wind brings clouds.

The wind also takes clouds away.

Clouds have many shapes.

What shapes do you see here?

Weather can change from day to day.

Weather can change very fast.

How is the weather changing in the picture?

What is the weather like?

Make a chart like this.

Each day put a check on your chart.

How many times did the weather change?

| | | | | |
|---|---|---|---|---|
| MONDAY | | | | |
| TUESDAY | | | | |
| WEDNESDAY | | | | |
| THURSDAY | | | | |
| FRIDAY | | | | |
| SATURDAY | | | | |
| SUNDAY | | | | |

spring

summer

fall

winter

Weather may change slowly.

It may change with the seasons.

There are four seasons.

How are the seasons different?

The air becomes warmer in spring.
Many plants begin to grow.
Many flowers bloom.

Summer days are longer.

The days are warmer too.

Plants grow bigger.

It is a time for summer fun.

In the fall the days are cooler.

Some plants stop growing.

In some places the leaves change color.

Then they fall to the ground.

Winter is the coldest season.

In many places it snows.

The days are shorter in winter.

Many animals sleep through winter.

Some animals have moved to warmer places.

You wear different clothes for different seasons.

You do different things in different seasons.

What seasons do the pictures show?

The season is the same in these pictures.

What season do you think it is?

How is the weather different in each picture?

Why is the weather different?

Make a chart like this.

|  | SPRING | SUMMER | FALL | WINTER |
|---|---|---|---|---|
| CLOTHES |  |  |  |  |
| PLANTS |  |  |  |  |
| ANIMALS |  |  |  |  |
| ACTIVITIES |  |  |  |  |

Cut out pictures to show how seasons are different.

# Check It Now

**WORDS TO KNOW**

What season is it?

Match the pictures with the words.

summer    spring    fall    winter

Which word do you need?

Use each word once.

wind  longer  seasons  flowers  coldest

Many ____ begin to bloom in spring.

In summer the days are ____.

There are four ____.

Winter is the ____ season.

The ____ moves the clouds.

158

# IDEAS TO KNOW

Look at the picture.

Name three things that do not belong there.

# USING IDEAS

Clouds move across the sky.

They change shape as they move.

Look at the clouds in the sky.

What shapes do you see?

Draw the cloud shapes.

Glue cotton to your cloud shapes.

# 10. Caring for Yourself

These boys and girls are in first grade.

They do many things each day.

They do things to stay healthy.

What do you do to stay healthy?

Tanya gets up early for school.
She washes her hands and face.
She gets dressed.
Her mother brushes her hair.

Eric gets up early, too.

Before school he eats a good breakfast.

This is what Eric ate today.

What did you have for breakfast today?

After breakfast Eric brushes his teeth.

Tanya likes to walk to school.

She is careful when crossing the street.

She waits until the guard tells her to cross.

Eric rides the school bus to school.

He waits for the bus by the curb.

Eric obeys the bus rules.

He does not stand up in the bus.

He does not shout or talk loudly.

Do you walk to school?

Do you ride a school bus?

What are some safety rules for walking?

What are some bus rules?

Make a chart like the one below.

| Some Safety Rules | |
|---|---|
| Walking to school | Riding the bus |
| | |
| | |
| | |
| | |
| | |
| | |
| | |

Eric and Tanya like to go to school.

They learn to read and write.

They listen to their teacher.

Learning is hard work.

It can also be fun.

What do you learn in school?

Your body needs exercise.

Exercise helps your muscles grow strong.

These girls and boys are in gym class.

What parts of their bodies are getting exercise?

Schoolwork can make you hungry.

Tanya buys her lunch at school.

Eric brings his lunch from home.

Eating a good lunch keeps you healthy.

Why are these good lunches?

Schoolwork can also make you tired.

Do you rest in school?

These children are having a rest.

Tanya has a snack when she gets home.

Then she goes outside to play.

Playing in the fresh air is good for her.

What do you do after school?

Now it is time for dinner.

Tanya washes her hands before dinner.

Work and play make Tanya hungry.

Tanya eats all the food on her plate.

The food she eats will help her to grow.

Find pictures of foods that are good for you.

Plan one meal.

What meal did you plan?

Healthy bodies are clean bodies.

Eric likes to take a bath.

He takes his bath at night.

He also brushes his teeth.

Eric worked and played hard.

He is tired from a busy day.

He will sleep about 10 hours.

Sleep helps his body get the rest it needs.

Tomorrow he will be ready for another day.

# Check It Now

**WORDS TO KNOW**

Which meal is it?

Match the pictures with the words.

breakfast    lunch    dinner    snack

Which word do you need?

Use each word once.

hands    grow    clean    brush    muscles

Exercise helps keep your ____ strong.

You should always wash your ____ before eating.

Healthy bodies are ____ bodies.

Food helps you ____.

You should always ____ your teeth after eating.

## IDEAS TO KNOW

Draw a picture for each sentence.

- Sit on the bus and talk softly.
- Listen to the guard when crossing the street.
- Exercise helps your muscles grow.
- Playing outside is healthy and fun.

Look at each picture.

Put the pictures in order.

## USING IDEAS

Draw a bathtub and a child.

Cut them out.

Glue the bathtub to a sheet of paper.

Put the child in the bathtub.

Color your picture.

# SCIENCE WORDS

## A

**air**  Air covers the earth. You cannot see or taste air.

**animal**  An animal is a living thing that can move on its own. A lion is an animal.

## B

**Big Dipper**  The Big Dipper is a group of stars that make a picture in the sky.

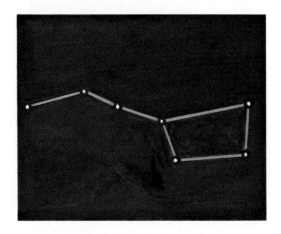

## C

**cloud**  A cloud floating in the sky is made of tiny drops of water.

**colors**  Red, blue, and yellow are colors.

**crater** A hole in the ground shaped like a bowl is a crater. The moon has many craters.

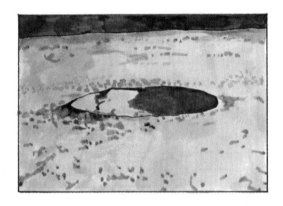

**E**

**ears** You use your ears to hear things.

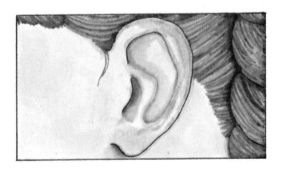

**earth** The earth is a round object made up of land and water.

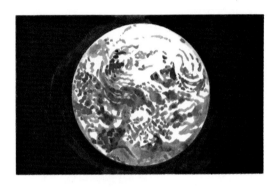

**egg** A bird hatches from an egg.

**exercise** Running and swimming are two kinds of exercise.

**eyes** You use your eyes to see things.

**F**

**fall**　Fall is the season in which many leaves change color.

**feathers**　Birds have feathers covering their skin.

**fur**　Many animals are covered with soft hair called fur.

**G**

**globe**　A round ball with a map of the world on it is called a globe.

**grow**　People, animals, and plants grow.

**I**

**ice**　Frozen water is called ice.

**L**

**land**   Land is part of the earth made of rocks and soil.

**leaf**   A leaf is a flat green part of a plant.

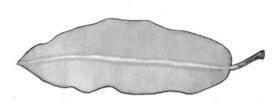

**living things**   People, animals, and plants are living things.

**M**

**moon**   The moon is the biggest object in the nighttime sky.

**move**   Things that move change place. Cars move.

**N**

**nose**   You use your nose to smell things.

**O**

**oceans** An ocean is a great body of water covering the earth's surface.

**P**

**pet** A dog is a good pet.

**plant** A plant is a living thing. Many plants have roots, stems, and leaves.

**pull** The boy had to pull the door shut.

**push** The boy had to push the door open.

**R**

**rock** A piece of stone is called a rock.

**root**  The part of a plant that grows down into the soil is called a root.

**S**

**seasons**  The seasons are spring, summer, fall, and winter.

**seed**  A seed grows into a plant.

**senses**  Seeing, hearing, tasting, touching, and smelling are senses.

**shape**  The ball has a different shape than the box.

 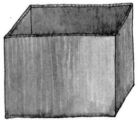

**shell**  A snail has a hard shell.

**size**  The size of the house may be big or small.

**skin**   Your skin can feel things.

**sky**   The sky is light during the day. The sky is dark at night.

**soil**   Plants need soil in which to grow.

**sound**   The drum made a loud sound.

**spring**   Spring is the season in which many plants begin to grow.

**star**   A star is one of the objects in the nighttime sky. Stars give off light.

**stem**   A stem is the part of a plant above the ground that holds the leaves.

**summer**   The days are warmer and longer in summer.

**sun**   The earth gets light and heat from the sun.

**T**

**tongue**   You use your tongue to taste things.

**W**

**water**   Water is found in oceans, rivers, lakes, and ponds.

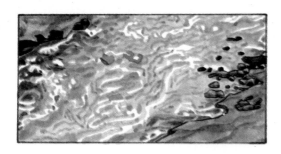

**weather**   The weather tomorrow will be warm, rainy, and windy.

**wind**   Moving air is called wind.

**winter**   The days are shorter and colder in winter.

# CREDITS

**Cover:** Taylor Oughton
**Other art:** Leigh Grant, Rebecca Merrilees, Taylor Oughton, Ed Valigursky

**Chapter 1** vi: *l.* Silver Burdett; *t.r., b.r.* Victoria Beller-Smith. 1: *t.l., b.r.* Silver Burdett; *b.l., t.r.* Victoria Beller-Smith. 2: Silver Burdett. 3: *t.* Silver Burdett; *m.l.* E.R. Degginger; *b.l.* Alvis Upitis/Shostal Associates; *b.r.* © Guy Gillette/Photo Researchers, Inc. 4: Pensy Brown; *inset* Dan De Wilde for Silver Burdett. 5: Dan De Wilde for Silver Burdett. 6: Silver Burdett. 7: *t.* John Shaw/Bruce Coleman; *m.l.* E.R. Degginger; *b.l.* G. Martin/Bruce Coleman; *b.r.* Hans Pfletschinger/Peter Arnold, Inc. 8–9: Silver Burdett. 9: *t.* © 1985 Elihu Blotnick/Woodfin Camp & Associates; *b.* Steve Pradon/Taurus Photos. 10: Silver Burdett. 11: *t.l.* Scott Ransom/Taurus Photos; *m.l.* Mary Bloom/Peter Arnold, Inc; *b.l.* Stephen Krasemann/Peter Arnold, Inc.; *t.r.* Richard Weiss/Peter Arnold, Inc.; *b.r.* Lionel Atwill/Peter Arnold, Inc. 12: Peter Byron for Silver Burdett, courtesy Tony's Pizza, Morris Plains, N.J. 13: *t.l.* Pensy Brown; *b.l.* E.R. Degginger; *t.r.* Peter Byron for Silver Burdett; *b.r.* Robert Dunne/Bruce Coleman. 14: Silver Burdett. 15: *t.l.* Sal Giordano; *b.l.* Thomas Hovland/Grant Heilman Photography; *t.r.* Mary Bloom/Peter Arnold, Inc.; *b.r.* Kenneth Fink/Bruce Coleman. 16–17: Silver Burdett. 18: John Running/Stock, Boston; *b.* Silver Burdett. 19–21: Silver Burdett.

**Chapter 2** 26: *l.* E.R. Degginger; *r.* Dan De Wilde for Silver Burdett. 27: S. Rannels/Grant Heilman Photography. 28: Silver Burdett. 30: *t.* Silver Burdett; *b.l.* Dan De Wilde for Silver Burdett. 31: Dan De Wilde for Silver Burdett. 32: *t.* F. R. Degginger/Bruce Coleman. *b.* Silver Burdett. 33: Silver Burdett. 34: *t.l.* E.R. Degginger; *b.l.* Breck P. Kent; *t.r.* Silver Burdett; *b.r.* Eric Kroll/Taurus Photos. 35: Dan De Wilde for Silver Burdett. 36: *l.* Gilbert Grant/Photo Researchers, Inc.; *t.r.* © Karlene Schwartz/Photo Researchers, Inc.; *b.r.* © Patricia Caulfield/Photo Researchers, Inc. 37: *l.* © Harald Sund; *t.r.* Jacques Jangoux/Peter Arnold, Inc.; *b.r.* Frank Pedrick/Visualeyes. 38: Silver Burdett. 39: *t.* Hickson-Bender Photography for Silver Burdett; *t. inset* © Dan Guravich/Photo Researchers, Inc.; *b.l.* Hickson-Bender Photography for Silver Burdett; *r.* Breck Kent.

**Chapter 3** 44: *t.* Wardene Weisser/Bruce Coleman; *b.* Peter Vandermark/Stock, Boston. 45: *t.l.* Scott Ransom/Taurus Photos; *m.l.* Breck P. Kent; *b.l.* © Mark Boulton/National Audubon Society Collection/Photo Researchers, Inc.; *t.r.* Bob and Clara Calhoun/Bruce Coleman; *b.r.* R.S. Virdee/Grant Heilman Photography. 46: *t.l.* Breck P. Kent; *b.l.* E.R. Degginger; *t.r.* Norman Myers/Bruce Coleman; *b.r.* Grant Heilman Photography. 47: *t.l.* © J.H. Robinson/Photo Researchers, Inc.; *m.l.* © Russ Kinne/Photo Researchers, Inc.; *b.l.* E.R. Degginger; *t.r.* Breck P. Kent; *b.r.* James Carmichael/Bruce Coleman. 48: *t.l.* Jen and Des Bartlett/Bruce Coleman; *b.l.* M.P. Kahl/Bruce Coleman; *t.r.* E.R. Degginger; *b.r.* © Stephen Dalton/Photo Researchers, Inc. 49: *t.l.* Z. Leszczynski/ Breck P. Kent; *m.l.* Frank Toman/Taurus Photos; *b.l.* Stephen Dalton/Photo Researchers, Inc.; *b.r.* R. Andrew Odum/Peter Arnold, Inc. 50: *l.* Stephen Krasemann/Peter Arnold, Inc.; *r.* © Bernard Wolff/Photo Researchers, Inc. 51: E.R. Degginger. 52: *t., b.l.* E.R. Degginger; *b.r.* Tom Brakefield/Taurus Photos. 53: Kim Taylor/Bruce Coleman; *inset* © Walter Ettarvey/National Audubon Society Collection/Photo Researchers, Inc. 54: *l.* Fred Bavendam/Peter Arnold, Inc.; *r.* E.R. Degginger. 55: *t.* E.R. Degginger; *b.* Jacques Jangoux/Peter Arnold, Inc. 56: *t.l.* © 1985 Fred Baldwin/Woodfin Camp & Associates; *b.l.* © Tomas Friedmann/Photo Researchers, Inc.; *t.r.* Stephen Krasemann/Peter Arnold, Inc.; *b.r.* Breck P. Kent. 57–58: Silver Burdett. 59: *t.* Linda Dufurrena/Grant Heilman Photography; *b.l.* E.R. Degginger; *b.r.* Frank Siteman/Taurus Photos. 60: *t.* Stephen Krasemann/Peter Arnold, Inc.; *b.l.* Silver Burdett; *b.r.* E.R. Degginger. 61: Silver Burdett.

**Chapter 4** 64–73: Silver Burdett. 74: © Lawrence Schiller/Photo Researchers, Inc. 75: *b.r.* Jerry Howard/Stock, Boston; *t.r.* Cary Wolinsky/Stock, Boston; *l.* E.R. Degginger. 76: Dan De Wilde for Silver Burdett. 77: Hickson-Bender Photography for Silver Burdett.

**Chapter 5** 80: *t.* Silver Burdett; *b.* Judi Benvenuti/Taurus Photos. 80–81: Summer Productions/Taurus Photos. 81: *t.* Tom Pix/Peter Arnold, Inc.; *b.* Silver Burdett. 82: *l.* Stephen Krasemann/Peter Arnold, Inc.; *t.r.* Rodder/Peter Arnold, Inc.; *b.r.* © Michael Manheim/Photo Researchers, Inc. 83: © Leonard Lee Rue III/Photo Researchers, Inc.; *inset* © Jerome Wexler/Photo Researchers, Inc.; 84: Silver Burdett. 85: *t., b.* E.R. Degginger; *r.* © Stephen Dalton/Photo Researchers, Inc. 86: *l.* Russell Bronson/Black Star; *t.r.* Steve Behal/International Stock Photo. 87: Dan De Wilde for Silver Burdett. 88: *t.l., b.l.* E.R. Degginger; *r.* © Gary Guisinger/Photo Researchers, Inc. 89: © Mike Lugne/Photo Researchers, Inc. 90: Silver Burdett. 91: NASA. 92: *l.* Robert P. Carr/Bruce Coleman; *t.r.* Mary Bloom/Peter Arnold, Inc.; *b.r.* Jane Burton/ Bruce Coleman. 93: *t.* Silver Burdett; *b.* Hickson-Bender Photography for Silver Burdett.

**Chapter 6** 96: *t., b.* E.R. Degginger. 96–97: Robert Frerck for Silver Burdett. 97: *t.* Bill Staley/West Stock; *b.* Silver Burdett. 98: Silver Burdett. 99: *t.l., t.r.* Dan De Wilde for Silver Burdett; *b.* Silver Burdett. 100: *t.* Timothy O'Keefe/Tom Stack & Associates; *b.* © Douglas Miller/West Stock. 101: Silver Burdett. 102: *t.* Mike Mazzaschi/Stock, Boston; *b.* Stuart Allen/Black Star. 103: Silver Burdett. 104–105: Hickson-Bender Photography for Silver Burdett. 106: *l.* E.R. Degginger; *t.r.* Owen Franken/Stock, Boston; *b.r.* © Charles Gordon/West Stock. 107: Dan De Wilde for Silver Burdett.

**Chapter 7** 110: *b.l., b.r.* Silver Burdett. 111: *t.l.* © John Sullivan/Photo Researchers, Inc.; *t.r.* Silver Burdett. 112: Silver Burdett. 113: NASA. 114: *t.* © Tom McHugh/Photo Researchers, Inc.; *b.* Silver Burdett. 115: Silver Burdett. 116: *l.* Bill O'Connor/Peter Arnold, Inc.; *inset* Kevin Gale/Taurus Photos; *r.* © Farrell Grehan/Photo Researchers, Inc. 117: E.R. Degginger. John Running/Stock, Boston. 118: *l.* William Eastman/Tom Stack & Associates; *t.r.* Peter Arnold; *b.r.* E.R. Degginger. 119: Dale/Johnston/Tom Stack & Associates. 120: *t.l., b.l.* Silver Burdett; *r.* Clyde Smith/Peter Arnold, Inc. 121: E.R. Degginger; *inset* Charles Kennard/Stock, Boston. 122: *l.* Silver Burdett; *r.* Imagery. 123: Eric Carle/Shostal Associates. 124: *t.* © Fred Lombardi/Photo Researchers, Inc.; *b.l.* Brian Parker/Tom Stack & Associates; *b.r.* Dave Woodward/Taurus Photos. 125: *l.* Brian Fox/Taurus Photos; *b.* Donald Dietz/Stock, Boston.

**Chapter 8** 128: Tom Stack & Associates. 129: *t.l.* Tom Stack & Associates; *t.r.* Tersch Enterprises; *b.* Kazuhiko Mori/Taurus Photos. 130: *t.* © Harald Sund; *b.* Tom Stack & Associates. 131: Tom Stack & Associates. 132: *l.* Lynn Bodek; *t.r.* E.R. Degginger; *b.* Silver Burdett. 133: E.R. Degginger; *inset* Hickson-Bender Photography for Silver Burdett. 134: © Harald Sund. 135: Silver Burdett. 136: Tersch Enterprises. 138–139: NASA. 140–141: Tersch Enterprises.

**Chapter 9** 144: Mildred Vortruba/Tom Stack & Associates. 144–145:© Katrina Thomas/Photo Researchers, Inc. 145: *t.r.* Cliff Moore/Taurus Photos; *b.* © Guy Gillette/Photo Researchers, Inc. 146: *l.* Charles Schmidt/Taurus Photos; *r.* Richard Perrine/Taurus Photos. 147: Gerald Corse/Tom Stack & Associates; *t.r.* G. Cloyd/Taurus Photos. 148: Werner Stoy/Bruce Coleman. 149: Silver Burdett. 150: Breck P. Kent. 151: Steve Raye/Taurus Photos; *t.r.* E.R. Degginger. 152: E.R. Degginger; *t.l.* Glenn Short/Bruce Coleman. 153: John Shaw/Tom Stack & Associates; *inset* E.R. Degginger. 154: E.R. Degginger; *inset* W. Garst/Tom Stack & Associates. 155: *t.* Pam Hasegawa/Taurus Photos; *t.l., b.l.* E.R. Degginger; *b.r.* Charles Schmidt/Taurus Photos. 156: *l.* Stuart Cohen/Stock, Boston; *r.* D.P. Hershkowitz/Bruce Coleman. 157: Silver Burdett, courtesy The Hillside School, Livingston, N.J.

**Chapter 10** 160: *l.* John Lei/Stock, Boston; *r.* Silver Burdett. 161: *t.l., t.r.* Dan De Wilde for Silver Burdett; *b.r.* Silver Burdett. 162, 164, 167 *r.,* 168 *l.,* 169 *l.,* 170 *t.,* 171–172: Dan De Wilde for Silver Burdett. 163, 167 *l.,* 168 *b.,* 169 *r.,* 170 *b.,* 174–175: Victoria Beller-Smith for Silver Burdett. 165: © Susan McCartney/Photo Researchers, Inc. 166, 173: Silver Burdett.